BURIED TREASURE

Addline Bova
Buried Treasure

Published by BooxAi

ISBN: 978-965-578-007-9

DISCLAIMER

This book contains Adult Content, such as pornography, sex, violence, or use of drugs, which are not appropriate for children's exposure.

BURIED TREASURE

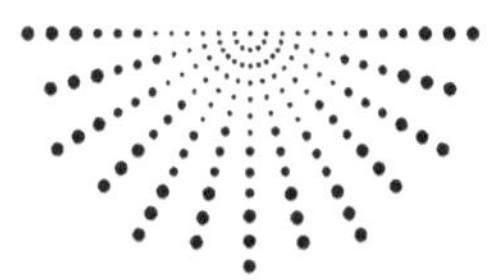

ADDLINE BOVA

Preface by
MIRKO PAVLEK

CONTENTS

PREFACE

Dissociative Identity Disorder (DID), formerly known as Multiple Personality Disorder is characterized by two or more distinct personality states and recurrent, unexplained gaps in recall of everyday functioning (DSM V). It is believed to emerge as a defense against unbearable terror, caused by recurring and severe sexual, mental and physical abuse in childhood, where the fragile ego self splits, unable to cope with psychic pain. The fragmented selves become complex, multi-layered personality structure with distinct identities who have unique names, age and their own memory structures and thinking patterns. Those identities are referred to as Alters. The Alters are able to take control over the primary identity and cause loss of personal agency, gaps in memory and change in behavior of the individual.

Shortly after I started working with Addie in therapy, she would spontaneously shift into deep dissociative states and stay there sometimes for the duration of the whole session. She would come back and resume normal functioning as if nothing had happened. After some time, once trust was established, she confessed that she had many experiences where she would lose a sense of time and a sense of self. She shared a story of finding herself on the swing in the playground, not knowing how she got there, or a story of finding herself strangely dressed and with make-up, not knowing how that happened. Her husband confirmed that and shared his own accounts of similar events. At that point, I realized that Addie has DID, and we started introducing a trance state to explore alternate selves. Addie would easily go in the trance dissociative state but was not connecting verbally while in the trance state. On the other hand, nonverbal communication was very strong. I would respond to nonverbals by gently talking to Addie and in that way, I would stay connected to her. Her nonverbal feedback assured me that we were connected. Somewhere along the way, while we discussed that, the idea for Addie to start automatic writings was suggested, and she embraced it enthusiastically. The Alters and their secrets started emerging through writing. Some of them shy, some of them raw and detailed, some of them full of rage and hatred. Some of them would overlap in their stories, giving a different perspective of the same event. The awareness that they all belong to the same body and same soul became the common contextual framework and a goal that governed the process.

The "Buried Treasure" is the result of that process. Most of the writing was preserved in the original form with minimal editing in order to portray a realistic experience of a fragmented and confused mind with overlapping memories.

The following is her and her Alters story.

Mirko Pavlek, LCSW-R

1

AUTUMN

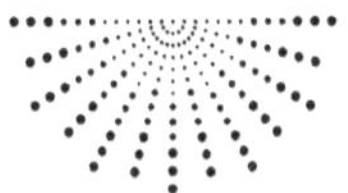

$\mathcal{A}$s miserable and traumatic as it was, I would not have changed anything that happened in my first eighteen years of life. Each action was a result of some other and then the end was finally the end. The only difference is that I wanted my heart and brain to forget what my remaining body had endured. My story was my own and FINALLY, someone was willing to listen. Praise God someone was willing to help me clear my brain of the misery. Little did I know that my heart was taking care of itself.

My choice to continue telling my story led to the severing of the vicious chain of events from being repeated in another generation. I was not going to be the next animal to terrorize a young person. I chose to tell anyone that would listen until I did not have to carry the memories around with me for the rest of my life. That is when I found Sam. He listened without judgement and helped me to unload the clutter and to let it go. There is still some work to do, but I am confident that it will get done. Every person on earth, I believe, was placed here for a purpose. The extent of my purpose, I do not know, and only time will tell.

I was born at Moses Ludington Hospital in Ticonderoga, NY, in the summer of nineteen sixty-nine. I was the second child to my mother, Babette. I was the first and only between my mother and my biological father. Now you may need to grab a pen and paper because my family tree has many branches and is very confusing. I went home with my mother to a one-bedroom apartment on Grace Avenue, Montcalm Street, or somewhere in between, I think. I do have a very vague memory of sharing her bed at that place, but not sure since I was also just getting around at that point on my incredibly young feet.

I say that I was the second child to my mother as she, at the time of my birth, had a son, Robert, who was born profoundly retarded and was newly institutionalized in Tupper Lake, NY. I then did not know about him. It was much, much later that I did. Robert was a result of a relationship with my stepfather's brother. It was fifteen or so years before I met him. Any earlier would have been inappropriate since speaking of anyone that is "retarded" was considered taboo.

My mom and biological father had a relationship that was less than ethical as my father was already married. The story that is told is that I was conceived behind a cemetery vault during a "play date." My father, by this time, had been married awhile to another woman and had three boys and one daughter already that I knew then about. I still do not understand. I think of myself as a product of a careless circumstance since there did not seem to be any love between them. He came and went as he wanted. I truly did not know about him until I was in Junior high school. Then only because he helped to buy my prom dress, never did he show any interest in getting to know me.

My step monster was incarcerated in Dannemora State Prison until nineteen seventy for a period of nine years for child molestation of a young girl that I later learned that I knew. On his discharge, he came to live with my mother and soon married on August twentieth, nineteen seventy-one. My only memory was being taken to my Aunt Freda's house in Fort Ann, NY so that she could babysit while Mom and Damian went on a "honeymoon." Nine months later, my sister was born.

My step monster, Damian, must have been on parole because I remember a man coming to my house – his name was Mr. Duckworth. He was a very tall and balding man with a deep and intimidating voice. When he came, he always wore a nice suit, and his visits were brief. I wonder if he ever asked about the relationships with the children around Damian. I still do not understand how he could have been on parole after a crime of hurting children and being married and living with two little girls. But he did. Yet another not-so-secure loop in the justice system.

Stories from my mother also were told where she and Damian would "have to" sell my crib and other baby essentials for rent money, or cigarettes, whatever the need was at the time. I am so glad that I do not remember. During this time, we lived in a trailer. It was also during this time that I would get cigarette burns on my thighs and butt from him.

My next memory was living on Grace Ave across from a hairdresser on a dead-end street. This is where mom would go for her "poodle perm." A very curly style that held snug to her head. This is the way she wore her hair for most of her life, unless she did not have money to pay to have it done. Our house was an apartment house where we lived downstairs. It was Mom and Damian, Amelia, and me. There was an apartment upstairs where Walt and Ivy lived. Ivy was crippled with arthritis and Walt was her husband and took care of her. She never left. She could not. I do not remember much about them, but I know that they could get moody, and it was my impression that they really were not kid lovers, but they tolerated them.

It was the time of the bicentennial as I remember the year Nineteen Seventy-Six from a quick visual of the calendar that then hung on the kitchen wall. Lots of things happened at that house. Mom had a miscarriage. Another brother, so she said. I remember the day only of tears and not much conversation. I was five, and Amelia was three. Most days there were less than pleasant. This is when I first remember terrible things happening to us, or at least me. I remember an evening when we had to go to bed at four o'clock so that mom and Damian could go out. We were left with a babysitter. To this day, I do not know who since we never saw them. We were not allowed to go to the bathroom once we got in bed, no reason, we just could not do it. If we did, we would have a slap or two waiting for us. Fear took over and survival was what it was. We went to the bathroom in the corners of closets, corners of rooms, sat on window ledges and let it go, anything not to have to go past them.

Mom and Damian portrayed the impression that they were avid pet lovers. Tippy was a cocker spaniel that we acquired from some unknown source. The only thing that I remembered was that Tippy was tied to the front porch by a short leash and had some sort of seizure and strangled himself. Tippy was replaced by a little black dog who, long story short, froze to death because he was tied by a short leash to the front steps in subzero weather. Then there was a grey cat. He ran away because he figured out that he was being fed rat poison. It goes on and on and on.

The inside of the house always seemed dark and cold and anything but a home. It was a box of wood where we put our heads at night. I do not recall any occasions of eating together as a family, playing in the yard, or seeing any friends.

I never did like being home. Amelia knows but does not tell because he does special things for her at my expense. "Daddy, don't make me ride Autumn naked around the house." "Daddy, can I have a ..." of course, he gave it to her.

He locked my door from the outside so that I could not run away. I heard the keys and knew what he wanted from me. He came over and ripped off the sheets and unzipped his pants. I pled, "Daddy, please don't, it hurts very badly." I tried to scream, and he covered my mouth. He looked at me and, in his breathless voice, asked, "Does it feel good?" I looked at him, not really seeing him and shook my head yes. I really did not feel a thing. I am numb.

So, on Lake George Avenue, this was a little house. Across the street from the "Beehive," another huge, haunted-looking house where Uncle Earl, or Aunt Ruthie, or someone lived. A huge house with a long drive. The house had no real color, just faded wood that was splintering. I was four years old. A very vague memory, though. This house had mice, smelled old and musty.

In my house, it was amazing how convenient the coloring books and crayons were when Child Protective Services would pull in the drive. We were never permitted to color. CPS said that there had been some reports and their purpose for being there and then they were soon gone. Secrets remained secrets. I do not understand why they never asked us. It was like they had to make a visual based on a report of suspected abuse. We slipped through those cracks. I have no faith in that system.

Our secrets of abuse that were suspected by so many was yet again unfounded by the decision makers. We continued to be beaten with belts and freshly peeled branches from a tree. We continued to drink expired milk and eat beans from a can. Eating bread and having a drink of water in the middle of the day were not allowed. He used to wait at the bottom of the stairs when we asked to go to the bathroom. We begged for him not to hit us, but once we hit the bottom -step, we would get swatted all the way to the bathroom.

In this place we had two beds, where my sister and I could behave like kids when the elders were not around. We would run around the room and jump on the beds, all those things that kids did, as we were oblivious to the fact that they could hear us. Usually, they were not around because they were downstairs visiting with friends, sitting out in the front yard with family, whatever. I remember ghosts in the closet, or so I thought. I hated that room. We moved to the room across the hall. This one was wide open. When we did get "caught" though, it was hell to pay.

We lived on Schuyler Street, the house where I did most of my growing up, the house where I remember the sexual abuse starting. I remember being fondled in the bathtub on school nights when Damian would give us a bath, because mom was at Bingo. Sometimes with Amelia, sometimes not. This is how it started, from what I remember.

I remember sleeping in a double bed with my sister. We spent a lot of time in that bed. We came home from school at two-thirty in the afternoon from school, ate dinner at three and went to bed by four-thirty. The sun was still out. We would fall asleep and wake up thinking it was a new day, only to find that it was a couple of hours later. Most nights mom would go to Bingo on the money that she borrowed, or that should be buying bread and milk, or whatever else to get us by for the month because that is how welfare paid us. We got food stamps and a check every first of the month. When mom went to Bingo, Damian would come and lay between Amelia and me. Usually, he would lie facing me so that he could touch me and make me touch him. My sister would either be asleep or at least be faking it; I do not know how much she remembers.

It was crazy how much I could do when I said yes to him. Why did I ever say yes, I do not know? That is why I said yes, although it was not like I had a choice. Sometimes I think that the punishment would be easier than the touching. I would be allowed to watch TV, which was never allowed otherwise. We could play outside, go to the store, and visit friends. It depended on how happy he was at the time. Of all those people that we visited, friends, neighbors, doctors, school, and the hospital, why didn't they ask, better yet, why didn't I tell? There were several times when I did tell. I told Margaret, Jo, Mom... the therapist. Nobody helped. I could not even help myself. Nobody would let me.

We were forced to sit on the floor with our backs toward the TV while they watched. We sat with legs out straight and with our hands on our knees and if we were to move, we would get swatted. I remember one time when I had to sit in my corner of the living room, out of sight of the television, by the door. That corner was very drafty, enough to cause me to get pneumonia and to get a rest in the hospital for a few days, thanks to Doc Shuler.

Our house had an open concept with a half wall separating the living room and kitchen. There were times that Damian would make me go with him behind the wall so that he could have sex with me. He would ejaculate and then urinate inside of my rectum. It was painful and degrading as I went into the bathroom, his urine would fall out of me onto the floor. The entire time, he was laughing heartily. I hated him. I would miss ambulance calls because he would not "let me go." At that point, I was an ambulance attendant with the local rescue service. My sister would have to sit on the other side of the wall. Damian made himself think that she could not hear, and she learned enough to try to coax me to say yes to whatever he asked. Then, of course, there was the basement when mom was home and he needed "something." Mom either played ignorant or was truly that she did not know or want to believe what was happening.

When it was not in my house, there were some bushes near the rescue building, the skating rink building down the road, my summer workplace... Wherever. The skating rink was the most convenient for him. It was an abandoned building where nobody went except to party and destroy the place, I would have to kneel or lay in broken glass, later to explain the injuries in the most convincing way possible.

We would occasionally act out his fantasies on his command. There would be times when Amelia and I would have to ride each other's backs in our underwear. My sister got exceptionally good at reverse psychology if she thought it would benefit us. For example, she would say "don't make Autumn take her clothes off, or don't make Autumn go with you." His response, of course, would be to make me do as she had indirectly asked. This guaranteed us a treat, or privilege. Sometimes it was a good dinner like Chef Boy R Dee or some sort of a sandwich. A walk to his friend's house, whatever it was, was better than what we had.

Mom enjoyed Bingo. She liked it a lot. She begged for money from neighbors, businesspeople, stole from Damian, whatever just so she could go. Seven nights a week, she was gone, giving an all-access pass to my youth and future woman-hood. Mom got arrested for welfare fraud on at least one occasion that I know of. The police came to our house, put her in cuffs and took her away. A couple of hours later, she returned with a gift that would ruin my life more. A criminal record. That very night she went to Bingo again. Lesson not learned.

I went back to school and was teased when people realized that our family was supported by public assistance, and my mother was arrested for abusing it.

In the later part of nineteen eighty-five, I was assaulted and raped by a neighbor who does not deserve mentioning his name. The night and early morning were dark and the street was safe. I remember not wanting to go to work that morning. It was overwhelming, to say the least. I could hear him walking behind me. I remember trying to walk away. I was left in an alley for dead. What events that transpired there are not known to me consciously, but the fear was very real. He went to prison for some time. Not enough, but at least there was some justice. He got out on parole for a very brief time and did it again to a seventeen-year-old boy. He went back, and the same thing happened repeatedly. In the last part of last year, he got out again, but was out for only three months and was incarcerated again until at least two thousand and twenty-one for sexually assaulting two girls, aged twelve and fourteen.

After graduating high school, I started college immediately and graduated in nineteen ninety with a degree in Licensed Practical Nursing. The first step in checking off an item on my bucket list, is becoming an RN.

During the time of going to school, I also worked full time as a 911 Dispatcher because then, I was "of age", I had to pay four hundred dollars rent to stay in my eight by twelve room. At some point while living there, I realized that the sexual abuse had stopped. I wondered why. Did I do something wrong? Did someone finally wise up to the situation? I had no idea. Not that I was saddened by any stretch, simply curious. It never happened again. At least it did not happen physically.

The mental and emotional abuse never stopped. I was still called names and reminded of my paternity. As I grew older, I became increasingly liberated, but it did not come for free. The entire time I remained there. I worked but did not get to keep anything. My money was not mine. My space and life were still not mine.

In the summer of nineteen ninety, I moved out. I moved into the basement with Maggie at her mom's house. It served the purpose. I had a huge waterbed on one side of the room, and she had the same on the other side of the room. Marge was my best friend back then. She listened to me when I told her about the abuse that I had gone through. She was a counselor in child and family services.

I remember a time that she and I and Addie would stay in the camper, and I would just spill everything to them. At times it was comforting. I did not know what to expect when I was telling them. It was a cleansing of my mind, it was a wish that they do something to help me, I just do not know. Addie was also a loyal friend. I spent a lot of time at her house when I was not with Maggie. Addie and I are still.

My time at Maggie's did not last long. Her mother gave me six months to find a job, or I would have to leave. I moved out and into an apartment with Maggie in a garage apartment. It was a nice apartment with more than enough space. I worked as a nurse at a long-term care facility/rehab center. I had no extra money because I spent every working penny on food and rent, but it was well worth the freedom. Maggie soon became too much for my brain to handle. Too much drama with scenarios that I could not determine happened. Instinct says no, but I truly do not know.

Soon, I became close friends with Janet through friends at the EMS service that we belonged to. I have known her most of my entire life. Her parents knew my parental units. She was a person that I was not sure about at first because she was notice-ably quiet and forthright. She appeared stern with many opin-ions, whether you wanted it or not. One thing I do know is that yes, she is opinionated, but she will not lie to you, she will support you if she agrees with you, and she has your back should you need some help. We have been at odds a couple of times and each time, we reconnect. Janet and I shared several apartments together as well as me living at her house with her parents. One day her mom was menopausal, hormonal, some-thing. She said that I would have to leave for a reason that I care not to disclose because it was just that insane. Janet left with me. Janet, to this day, is my best friend. My sister is not related by blood. She is consistent, she loves my kids and cares about me. I feel the same about her. Her family became my family once my mother passed away. We eventually became housemates a few times and then I met Matthew and with him is where I stay.

I met the man of my dreams. He is far from perfect but perfect for me. He had a captivating smile and a personality that I knew I needed in my life. I interviewed him for an EMT posi-tion at the Great Escape, where I worked for about a year and a half as an EMT.

He walked in and his smile lit up the room. He was wearing a suit and was well-spoken and certainly ready for the inter-view. I remember that he talked and talked and talked for what seemed like forever. My first impression is that he was just a geek that spoke way too much. He grew on me.

Matthew was easy to get to know. He was very friendly, smart, attractive, and I liked him. I trusted him. Instinct, my gut said he was good. I had never felt that way before in my life. My mind was crazy because he was significantly younger than I and wondered "how that worked" these days. There are challenges, as in any marriage, but we are a great match. Apparently, works well for some because we have been married for fourteen years.

Matthew proposed on December thirty first in two thousand and two in Shepard's Park in Lake George. We were both sick with colds but went out anyway to have dinner and see Christmas lights in the town. We ate dinner at O'Tooles Restaurant and drove to Lake George. We parked and began our walk. We ended up in front of a park bench where we sat in the summertime. When he hugged me and began by saying "I don't want to be together like this anymore", and I was convinced that he wanted to break up with me. He needed a change. I looked at him again and he was on one knee and holding the ring that had changed my life forever. We were married on April eighth in two thousand and six.

Sam is a Licensed Clinical Social Worker and Certified Hypnotherapist that specializes in trauma. Matthew brought me to his session, tricked me into going to see him. On first impression, he is an interesting character, lots of stories, very smart. On the way out of the office, I took one of his brochures and learned more of his story. My respect grew. A man not intimidated by challenging work and appreciates the life that he is living.

I saw Sam for the first time, it was what was initially thought to be an "interview" of sorts so that Matthew and I could begin fine-tuning our marriage. Not that there were any issues, communication, and intimacy on occasion. I knew that if Sam wanted to climb my family tree, our fine-tuning would be placed on hold for a while because my past was about to slap me in the face, again.

We talked about my family tree, as suspected. I gently explained to him that with the branches of my tree being so scattered, it is not one that I have been interested in climbing. He fetched a larger piece of paper. We began. Sam unaffected.

Mom and Dad were never married but continued to "carry on" well after I was a teenager. Damian was oblivious. He carried on his day-to-day routine as always. Amelia was the only child between Damian and Mom. I was the only child between Thomas and Mom. Robert was the only child between Mom and Damian's brother Robert. Eve, Mary, Caleb, Nolan, and Richard are Thomas's kids with Angel. Phew!!!

My relationship with Mom was complicated. She did what she felt would keep her secure, and not necessarily what was right. She knew about the abuse but chose to do nothing about it. Ignorance, fear, intimidation, I do not know, but she did nothing. She gambled seven nights a week. Bingo was her game of choice. She begged, borrowed, stole, and sold belongings of ours just so she could go. Even an afternoon in the police station did nothing after she had been arrested for welfare fraud. Complicated? I guess so. I am still at the question of "have you forgiven her?". I do not know.

When we got to Damian, it began. The short story of my relationship with him and why he remains my demon.

In our next session, I was introduced to a trance. Fascinating what capacity your subconscious must store things. My mind drifted off to places that I had not been to in a long time. I could feel a struggle between my rational mind and my subconscious. One was fighting the urge to talk about this demon inside me, and the other wanted to disclose information. My guess is that they concluded, and the struggle stopped. That night I had a dream about wanting to put my kids up for adoption because I could not care for them as I wanted or could. In this dream, no element surfaced that led me to believe that it was a dream.

Very real. I was able to rationalize and determine that I had to "get my stuff together" because they were mine and my priority.

Typically, I like to watch the news and then go to sleep, which tends to put me at about eleven-thirty in the evening. You would think that I would change that habit since I need to get up every morning at six. Last night was no different. A little before eleven-thirty, I snuggled down into my usual position and fell asleep. I did not even remember trying, since the two or three nights prior, I was busy coughing all night. Last night I had a Robitussin toddy. It really did seem to help. Anyways, the next I remember, Damian was chasing me. Everybody was around. Pooh, Janet, Matthew, a bunch of other people, not sure of where I was. I remember Pooh scooped me up and took me swiftly to the door. He told me that I was ok, that nobody was going to hurt me. I looked at him and believed him.

Things took a drastic change, and I am not sure of where I was, but Damian was there again. He had a look on his face, like he had the advantage. Evil. I tried to run, but he got me, and I looked down and I had some huge fleshy wounds on my lower legs, bleeding all over the place. He had stabbed me several times. Later to find out that he did it so that I could not run anymore. I looked away from the wounds and looked at Damian. The next second, I was on top of him. He was pinned to the ground by his neck. His face was turning colors, his neck veins were distended, and he had intense fear in his eyes. I was killing him. The same people that were protecting me were pulling me off him. I kept asking why. Why? I tried to tell someone that he had hurt me. I tried to show them. I was awoken to hear by the arrogance of my phone alarm clock. I remembered hearing the anchor on channel ten saying it is six eighteen in the morning and time for your morning traffic. A new day has started.

This whole dream was a bit crazy for me since Damian died on his birthday four years ago. Ironically, he died the same day that my mother, his wife, died in nineteen ninety-five. I had no need to think about him because he could not hurt me anymore. I was done trying to convince people that he was bad – it did not matter anymore.

So, in my dream last night, I was homeless.

I was young enough to be at home with Mom and Him, but he was the only person that I saw. I tried several times to physically knock him down, but for whatever reason, he kept getting back up. He yelled, although I did not hear a word that he said. It was like I was deaf.

I had a few of my personal things with me. I had my journal where I authored poems, thoughts, and other craziness in. Songs that I loved that made me feel happy or sad, depending on the feeling of the day. I had a couple of articles of clothes and that was it. I cried a lot in my dream. I was crying because I had no place to go. You would think that I would be happy because I got away from him, but I was not. Nobody wanted to ask me to stay with them. I met many people in my dream. Most of them I knew.

I owned three cars also. One was stolen, the other at his house, and finally, the other was at my disposal, but for another reason, I did not use it. I tried to make people hear me that I was homeless, but they laughed at me. My friend Ray bought me a Diet Pepsi, which is my absolute favorite. I cried some more because he was nice to me. Ray was later discovered to be missing and assumed dead in my dream. I found a job, sold one of my cars for additional money and then I woke up.

As a rule, I avoid attention. The only attention that I genuinely enjoyed was when I had babies and got married. I welcomed the attention because I felt beautiful.

I tend not to show myself attention, probably so that I do not draw attention to myself. I never ask for it.

I think of attention as more of a punishment. As a child, I longed for it. As a young girl, incest, molestation, sodomy, physical torture, and neglect were what I got in return. Asking for attention when I tried to tell people about my abuse proved ineffective.

Attention should be given to good people who do good things. Saying and affirming that I deserve attention sounds egocentric and selfish. It does not feel good. I wish someone would ask me about what others only speculate. I want to tell someone the truth about what happened. Today, I continue to attract the attention of my husband and children.

To be considered useful, I need to do something that someone needs. I take care of my kids and house - my husband brings feelings of value. Every night after dinner, he says "thank you". He encourages my kids to do the same.

In the job place, I liked my work as a nurse but I was replaced on the last two occasions because of performance or personality issues. I had never felt so useless before then.

I did so many things for many people. I have a tough time saying "NO" to anyone. I manage a nonprofit, fundraise for other organizations, they do offer a shimmer of hope for the future.

As a friend, I offer unconditional love and support to a chosen few. Fewer reciprocate. I feel like my value comes from satisfying the needs of other people.

Today I am not so sure of who I am. I went to Walmart to pick up Sarah's prescription and almost signed someone else's name. Who does that? I slapped Sarah to grab her attention. I never do that. I caught myself doing things that would otherwise offend others. Is this another alter that could be showing their little self? A rebel of sorts?

I absolutely HATE waking up in the morning and not knowing who I will be for the day. Of course, my first choice is me, Addie. Why can I not just be Addie for an entire day?

This morning, I woke up mad as hell. I do not know why, but Matthew said that I was kicking and screaming in my sleep. I of course, do not remember anything. Throughout the day, I was not nice at times, and then others were great.

So, I messed up my appointment times with Sam. I really need to be prepared because missing these things does nobody any good. I am not in a good place these days. Last week, it was like watching myself from another dimension. I watched myself at the pharmacy while picking up pills for Matthew. I signed and almost did not know who to write on the credit card slip. If that can mean anything.

Matthew says that I am "Ho Hum" lately. I find my mind wandering, but when he asks what I am thinking of, I cannot recall. I am sad a lot. I stare into space a bunch and do not really see anything.

I saw an old friend who passed away several years ago in my dream. He was my prom date. We went as friends as for some reason that I only know now, we could be nothing else. He died of AIDS. He was gay and was quite precarious. He was a good guy, and I am happy that he wanted to stop by to say hello.

I am on a fiscal freeze that has me "fit to be tied". I am most happy when I am shopping. I have been a week without eating out. I feel like an addict of sorts. I can see how hard it is for someone who takes drugs or drinks, and who likes to eat a lot.

So, my first dream after my last session was a vague memory. It was an addition to a former dream. I have been having a dream about being held down by my throat. I look up and the dream goes black. This time, I am in the same scenario, except this time, I see him. He has me by the throat and using a hammer handle to sodomize me. I feel nothing.

I have yet to be able to become an active part of the dream. I am told that it is possible, though.

I had a dream. I had a dream that I was trying to leave my mother and Damian's house, but everything was stopping me.

I tried to get my personal things to leave, but I had to "make an appointment". I was already out, but not entirely. I made an appointment for the next day. Mom had an appointment to attend to, so she could not be there. I said no, I will wait for mom to be able to stay with me. It ended in a fight because mom felt that I was being childish. That I had something against him. WELL, I DID!!

I told her, as I had several times, that I was being abused, and yet nothing. I was continuously in conflict with both. I could never do what I wanted because there were always alternate plans for me. I woke up still struggling.

If there is anything that I look forward to in my life, it is changes. I would love to have been able to change my family dynamic when I was a child. It never happened. It changed for the bad. I would have to change my choices for school, but to live, I had to quit school to work, so that I could survive. I wanted to become an RN. Instead, I became an LPN that loves trauma. The choice was mine to be homeless and go to school. Or work and pay rent. So, I worked two full-time jobs and went to school. Sleep was a luxury. I did not get any. Much later and early into the new millennium. I went back to school and worked full time. I have a BS in Health and Human Service Management, now working on becoming a nonprofit for the recognition, education, and advocacy of people who are being abused, have been abused, or at risk for abuse. I am a survivor of fourteen years of child sexual abuse. I also have clinical depression/anxiety and Dissociative Disorder (formerly multiple personalities). I want to change my relationship with Amelia, but because of our own insecurities, it will never happen. It always defaults to an argument. Thomas, Eve, Paige, and Allison and the other two guys are questionable. The trust factor is not there for the guys, but I adore all three ladies.

The question should not be how I get to trust, it should be why I should trust. Life has its ugly head in a way that you get it, until you lose it. I trust the people that I am supposed to and where did that get me?

SO, why should I trust? Mom got someone else to sleep with, that man took my mom away and then he did dreadful things to me. Then, so did everyone else and then nobody did anything to help me.

This is the way that Sam tells me that I will one day reconnect with the disconnected part of me. I am sure that since she is still peeking and is hesitant to come to me that the trust is not there. I am now parenting three children. How do I parent myself like I parent my own babies?

I am feeling a bit ill today. Lots of fatigue and sniffles. Yesterday was weird too. I had a three hour long dental appointment. But the result was more than I could have asked for. I love my crown. I feel like I missed a portion of yesterday. I do not really remember taking the kids to school or going to. The night before, I was tired, a bit unraveled, and did not really have it together. I was sad that I was denied social security because it was felt that I could do something. I am fifty-one years old with a bachelor's degree and I can do SOMETHING!???

I was seventeen, worked at McDonald's and got fired because I lacked the motivation and energy required for the position, is what I was told. I was let go from Urgent Care because I was a "poor fit." I had my head in the clouds, to be exact. Both ends of the spectrum, and I did not cut it. I did call a lawyer who said that it is their job to deny and my job to appeal. I do not know if I have the energy.

I see flashes of Damian's face daily. Today, I brought in groceries from the car, and he said, "can I give you a hand"? I gasped, and he was gone. I see him when I hear hands brushing over whiskers of a man's beard, the chains of a trucker's wallet, when I smell stale smoke on clothes, when I see a man grin a little awkward, when I close my eyes to go to sleep....

Is this possible? I am beyond the possibility. Laundry is out of control, dishes are heaping over the sink, there is more hair than on a Pomeranian on the floor, we can't eat at the table, we can't sit in the Livingroom, I have to take the kids to the dentist, grocery shopping, buy a new shower nozzle, take the daughter to the ER, I have to take the kids to therapy, I have been putting off a PT appointment for my knees for quite some time, I have to declutter, Noah can't find his shoes, I can't find my soul, ...

I pray and pray every day that all will be good, I do not have the energy to do it alone anymore. How do I get them to understand?

I keep having the same dream periodically. In general, I am in some dire situation and need help, and nobody will help me. Last night, I was having some sort of a medical problem. I was on an ambulance stretcher being taken into a medical facility and I kept being sent back. I was being taken to a medical helicopter and I never got there. It was beyond reach.

I looked out the window seeing a werewolf staring back at me. Terrifying, at least. Going around the corner, I saw a strange display of Christmas cacti and poinsettias, candles, and memorabilia of some sort. It almost looked like a sanctuary, where someone would go to worship someone, or something. Around the next corner was Damian. He was sitting in front of the door that would let me out. He was not going to let me out. My baby girl, Sarah, was there. Then again, could it have been me? The entire scenario was moving in circles.

Aunt Janice was argumentative. Saying that she would pay fifteen hundred dollars for a place to live. What? Mom is looking for a job. I was looking for a job and a place to live.

"Werewolf – is a mythological creature that can transform from a man into a monster or vicious animal. In legends, a meeting with the werewolf portends nothing good. Man-werewolf after transformation turns into a scary bloodthirsty creature, dangerous and treacherous."

No place was safe. Every place was strange. I wanted no part of it.

Dream of mom lying on her bed. Mom often spent time in her bedroom when something bothered her. I went in and sat with her. She was quiet, answering questions without words, or not at all. I asked her what she was doing. She appeared deeply immersed in something. She insisted "nothing". Finally, after much questioning, she states that she is going to live with Uncle Willard. Uncle Willard was my grandmother's brother. I asked her why we had to go there. She looked at me and said that she was going alone. Why would mom leave without us?

Mom began to cry. I asked several times, finally getting the courage to ask if Damian was mean to her. The sobbing got louder, and her chest was heaving when she admitted that Damian was abusing her.

The fact that she was willing to leave her two kids alone with this evil man showed me the mom I never seen before. The weak and vulnerable side. It made me question her feelings for us. Was its self-preservation, was she running away because she did not have answers. Was she scared? I woke up pissed.

It is like going someplace, taking a nap, and waking up a bit disoriented, and quite possibly in a place that I never intended on being. Most of my "episodes" for the lack of a better word, happen when Emma, Lilly, Mae, or Rikki have decided that they would like to become an active participant in whatever I am doing. Driving the car, playing in the playground, sitting in a therapy session, sleeping at night...

I know, I know, they are all me. I am told that often. I know that each is a part of my life that represents me at various stages, or ages. I am mesmerized by how one part of my brain can turn me on to an entirely different view of my past. I have come to appreciate these "others" as me, I understand their purpose, but I doubt that I will ever totally understand how they just took over my life, now after fifty-two years. Was I really needing closure to begin to be the happy, enthusiastic, devoted person that I longed to be? I think so.

While I sleep, my alters feel safe to move around and feel secure. One of the ways they feel and communicate is in my dreams. I have done my share of sleepwalking and re-arranging things in my sleep, but if I am not sleeping alone. I guess, therefore, Matthew would get beat up so often. I would kick and scream in the middle of the night. When I wake up, I have no memory of the dream, usually.

Sometimes the dreams are graphic images of exactly what

happened in the past – quite possibly; these events are ones I held only in my subconscious for one of my alters to one day share, when the time is right. They are the security force for my conscious. I knew nothing about it because they shielded me from them and now, I have reached the stage where this secret should be kept from me no longer.

In other dreams, the actual circumstances featured have never occurred. They simply represent dilemmas and emotions that are of great significance to my alters. The biggest point, I guess, about either sort of dream is that they communicate things that are deeply distressing the alter and trying to bear them alone has become too great for the alter and is no longer necessary. The alter needs me, my support, and the support of other parts of me as well.

My head feels very crowded these days. I cannot be one hundred percent sure of who is there. My thoughts are incomplete, I am jumpy when Matthew kisses me, my dreams are becoming more vivid and memorable. Although, they are not making much sense.

I have been referred to as "off" by Matthew. I admit that I am but cannot really tell you why. My periods of "out of body" are more. I often feel like I am watching myself go through the day. My body moves and it is like I am not moving it. I seem to zone out more.

These past few weeks have proven to be non-productive. What do I want to do when I grow up? I do not know anymore. I am stuck in a rut. I feel like I am not sure of where to go in my recovery. I am stressed in that I do not want to provide for my family anymore. I am frustrated that what I do really does not feel good enough.

Rikki is more prominent again. She is not really saying anything, but is on guard. Mae is more in the foreground than the background, Emma is closer to Lily, and Lily is anxious, and wants to hide again.

I keep having this dream about Lily and she keeps singing

the words, "No, Victor." The only Victor that I remember is my Uncle Victor, who was married to my Aunt Kitty (Katherine). Aunt Kat was my grandmother's sister. She was killed in a car accident almost twenty years ago. Uncle Victor died a few years later of throat and esophageal cancer.

I remember going to Aunt Kat's house when I was young to play with Chipper and Cathy, who were my cousins. The memories are not very vivid, because I was so young. Uncle Victor started coming to my house after he and Aunt Kat got divorced. He was there a lot. He seemed genuinely nice. He was very affectionate. I remember when he whistled and tapped his fingers, it sounded like a parade. When we sat on his lap, he bounced us like we were on a horse. It was fun. Lily does not remember it that way.

So, this week coming, we are all on vacation. We came early to camp. I washed fifty loads of laundry (slight exaggeration), packed for three, shopped a bit, cleaned the kitchen so that we were ok on return. I will not be loaded down when we come back home. Granted, we are not going far, just camp, but I like to come home and not have a week's worth of work to do.

My mind is all over the place. Sometimes I remember things that need to happen, other times, no. I forgot that I needed to bring out the garbage that I cleaned the refrigerator into. I forgot the medication that Matthew says that he asked me to bring. I forgot my pillow that saves me from the wretched hot flashes at night, yadda yadda yadda. I forgot. Why?

My "time away" has increased. About an hour a day, sometimes more. My dark friend is unwilling to be confronted, my "society" is going about the day with me, bringing memories that I had tucked away for whatever reason.

I feel angry but I do not know why. Is it hormonal or psychological? I do not know.

I have had a few occasions where my mind does not know what my body is doing. Sometimes while walking, I will just change direction and wonder why. I will find myself in the car and wonder why.

This time, I am in Michael's. I love Michael's. Just looking. I did not want to buy anything, just look. I am walking with a cart just in case I find something. My cart just spontaneously started going in the wrong direction. I thought it was just a bad cart, so I switched. The next cart did the same thing. This time, the cart rammed into a display of crafting beads, knocking them over. There were beads all over the place. I heard a chuckle in my head. I tried to stop and help but could not. My cart and body went straight and soon after, rolled a display of yarn into the back of the store. Again, a chuckle in my head. By the time I got it together, I was mortified by what I am sure that the store employees thought of me. I apologized many times as I stopped at the beads to assist with the display and left before being asked to.

I am having some crazy dreams about living in general. One does not make any sense at all. It reoccurs often. I am in a war zone and have been taken over by an enemy. They are everywhere, carrying huge guns and yelling. Incomprehensible, and I am sure not good things to all that listen.

I am lying on the ground in a ditch. I am very still with my eyes open and fixed. I figured out that I was playing dead to avoid getting killed. I am being stepped on and kicked, I am numb and do not flinch. I wake up.

I wake up drenched in sweat, looking around and trying to figure out where I am. My heart is racing, and I feel like I will soon die. I hear my husband's Bi Pap; I feel the dog's breath on my hand. I am good.

An even more frequent dream is drowning and not being able to breathe. I am facing down in a body of water. It starts this way. I remember that I am holding my breath to the point of struggle. When I start to lose the struggle, I wake up. I am gasping for air, I am sweaty, my heart is racing, I feel like I have died. Again, it takes a bit to recover, BUT I do and wait for a second and try to reorient myself. Jeter is always there. Matthew is next to me, asleep; I can hear my daughter's television. It is good. I can breathe.

My society has been active lately. From moving the yarn to knocking over beads to bringing flashes of my past when I least expect it. I see flashes of faces and places that I recognize but cannot figure out why. They do not go together.

Why? Sam is asking. What are the triggers? I am not sure of specifics, but I can tell you the ones that I know about.

If I smell stale cigarette smoke, If I smell body odor or sweat, see a man wearing revealing clothes, trucker wallets, dirty worn jeans, men looking at me intently, breathing other than my own near me. I feel extremely anxious when Matthew comes up behind me and kisses my neck. If I see a news story about violence, if I hear conversations about domestic abuse or violence. I find myself profiling while dropping my son off at school with the rest of the parents. The dark, basements, the smell of musty fabric, the sound of water dripping in dark spaces... I am sure that there are more, and my list will continue.

For the past couple of days, I have felt like I am not alone. I feel like someone is watching me, although when I turn around, nobody is there. Except when I look in a mirror. I look in the bathroom mirror, and I see someone looking over my shoulder. The figure is black, as in like a dark shadow, and I cannot see facial features. This morning, it took me by surprise, as it took my breath away and made me panic. My heart was racing, I was sweating, I wanted to run, but there was no place to go. I turned around; nobody was there.

Almost feels like when I was telling of my abuse. Nobody would help me. No matter where I went or who I told, nobody was able (or willing) to help me.

Sonofabitchingmotherfuckingcocksuckingfuckface! It is like cookies and milk before bed. Like cold sheets after a long balmy day, a hot shower on a wintry night. Just feels good to scream!

Mr. Jim Croce said it best when he wrote "If I could save

time in a bottle, the first thing that I would like to do," is the go back to the day when Mom and I would be alone in the world. Damian would never be released from prison, and they would never have gotten married.

The pivotal moment was when they got married. The opportunity was there. Mom did not satisfy his needs, so he needed something else. Someone else. Me. I wanted to be transparent. I did not want to be seen by him. I hid a lot, but still got into trouble. I found that no matter what I did, I remained the one that would get the beating when I came down the stairs to go to the bathroom. Belt, sticks, coat hanger, fly swatter, lit cigarette, whatever was there, was what went across my backside.

Still, no matter what noise I made, nobody listened. So, I stayed quiet. I enjoyed being with Uncle Rick. He hated Damian. He hated that mom married him. He hated that I was getting beaten up. He was not the conventional guy, though. He was a vigilante who enjoyed taking care of things his own way. It was nothing for him to get into a fight with the guy next door for calling grandma a bad name. In my case, he did nothing. I stay quiet. I hide.

It seems that everything that I ever want to do, that all the others in school are doing, I never get to do. Usually, it is because I cannot leave their site. I am always punished for whatever reason. I go to the bathroom once I am in bed at four-thirty in the afternoon, I get a belt across the butt/lower back. I speak without being spoken to; I get a wet washcloth across the face. There was no playing stickball on the road until the streetlights came on with Jo and Evelyn, and Bill. There was no kickball in Jo's yard with the rest of the hood.

I snuck over the fence into the treehouse one day and I was confronted at the end of the ladder with Damian and a wet switching stick from the tree. For every time he told me to come down, I would get beaten with the stick harder and harder until, on a couple of occasions, I bled.

At four in the afternoon, when it is time for bed, if I speak, or if they hear me, I get a slipper, belt, fist, flyswatter, serving spoon, etc., across the arms, legs, butt. I never get all my home-work done. Of course, if you have the schedule that I did, day after day. There is no time. Of course, Damian wants us to go to sleep for when Mom goes to Bingo. He can then slide on into the bed without being noticed by anyone except for me. I cringe, I cry, I ask him to stop. Are you fucking deaf???

No baths, go to school with dirty, greasy hair and a bruised and dirty body. Wear the same clothes for the same week. I do sneak into the bathroom on occasion and take a small sponge bath and hand wash my underwear, though. Usually, when Damian forgets to lock my bedroom door from the outside.

Damian would repeat the same mantra over and over. "You are a worthless piece of skin. You are the bald eagle's daughter. You are not my daughter. You never will be." I am no good, I deserve this. After a bit, I tend to believe it.

"You are a big fat liar! Nobody believes you. It is my word over yours. You asked for everything you got. You are not my daughter. You cannot rape the willing. I was framed and put in prison. I spent nine years in lockup because of someone like you. I will kill you if you run your fucking mouth to anyone, do you understand me. you will never live."

"In my head, I could hear, "tell your bald little friend that you are sorry that you wasted his time and that you made it up. You are a liar who just wants some attention because mine was not good enough for you. He cannot help you because I will never go away. I will be in your head, I will be in your gut, I will forever be in your pussy. your beautiful little pussy."

Mom died in the summer of nineteen ninety-five at the age of fifty-two. She passed away alone in a hospital right in our hometown.

At the beginning of that year, I remember the day I returned to work from my lunch break at the health Center. I had never seen mom the way I did that day. She was sitting on the steps with her head down. I walked up to her and asked her what was wrong. She looked up at me and I could tell that she had been crying. "I'm dying, I have six months to live."

Mom was plagued with cirrhosis of the liver that she acquired from hepatitis when she had surgery that required her to have a blood transfusion. Her time with liver disease was stressful for all involved. Damian was in denial, one daughter lived an hour away, and the other was developmentally delayed in an institution. That left me, a quarter of a mile up the road. That was not a bother to me, really, because I am a firm believer that we should take care of the ones that take care of us. She did not always have my best interest in mind, but I am alive.

I took her to many doctors' appointments, managed many insurance papers, made funeral arrangements, helped to lift her off the floor and then the final ride to the hospital in my new car.

The last ride sticks in my head as though it was yesterday. She was obtunded and could barely move, but she was adamant about riding in my car. The ride to the hospital was quiet and by the time we got there, she was unresponsive. Her ammonia levels were extremely high, causing her altered mental status. I got her into the emergency room and parked the car. By the time I got back inside, nurses were attempting to pass a naso-gastric tube from her nose into her stomach.

The doctor stated that the only way to lower the ammonia levels was through the digestive tract into the colon and out into the feces. This would mean making her endure enemas frequently. Since mom was not able to make decisions, it meant that her husband would need to speak on her behalf. After much discussion, we decided that no, she would not be getting enemas, this would be the beginning of the end. She was admitted for palliative care. We called out the priest for her sacrament of the sick and held vigil by her bed. Days went by, I talked to her about everything. Sometimes we got a response, sometimes not.

My birthday came and I got a card and flowers when I turned twenty-five. I told her that I loved her, and she responded, "and I love you." Two weeks later, at ten twenty-five, we received the call that mom had passed away. When we went to the hospital, she looked so peaceful, but because of the cirrhosis, she cried yellow tears and her skin was weeping yellow.

I do miss my mother. She left a hole in my heart that really will never be filled. Regardless of what she did or did not do, she gave me life.

I sat here today; Matthew is still in Pittsburgh. I still have my head full of voices to keep me company. I am talking to Jeter like he is human. Most of the time, I forget that he is not. I laid on the floor with him. My heart is pounding, I am taking way too many deep breaths and my mind and body are racing too fast for comfort.

I laid on my back on his bed. He lays alongside me, licking tears from my face. I close my eyes and start my little process to see if it still works. I go through all five senses and see what I can do to calm down.

Sight. I see the many faces that keep me busy, I see the floaters that sometimes help me to fall asleep, I see darkness. I see him. I do not fully understand why it is that the flashbacks are coming more frequently, or that the time lost during my day is increasing, or that all my alters are feeling the need to talk.

Hearing. I am holding a day of conference tomorrow. Like a parent-teacher conference. Each will have their turn to tell me what is on their perspective minds. I hear idle jibber jabber. I cannot focus on one voice to listen to make sense of any content. I hear the washing machine in the distance. I hear the beating of my heart, whooshing in my ears. I hear some voices from the end of the house from some ghosts that stopped by to see how things were progressing. I hear the clock and the kitchen sink faucet sending a periodical drip into the drain. I hear Jeter licking and snoring, sighing, and attempting to talk to me. What a good boy.

Smell. I smell the stinky boy that is doing his best to keep me sane. I smell his feet that remind me of Doritos. I smell periodically, the smell of stale sweat, old cigarettes, and dirty clothes. I realize that these are flashbacks, the same as the face that stares into my eyes while raping my soul.

Feeling. I feel cold, then hot, I feel flushed, sweaty, my teeth chatter, I want to hide. I do not have to, but I want to. My body cannot stop moving. I am "popping my knuckles", something that recently just started, I am digging at my skin which is also very new. I am wringing my hands. I am swinging my feet. I have always done that. I am deep breathing; I am slowly finding my body is finding its resting point. I continue to breathe. I awoke to the alarm on my cell phone, it was time to get the boy.

A survivor is someone who withstood the trials of a situation. They stayed alive when others may have died. I am not yet a survivor, I still dream vivid dreams of him. I see the blood as it trickled down my legs into my panties and on the bed. I was lying and being a bad girl when I told mom that I had a bloody nose when she did the laundry. She would never think any different. I am still living it. He is dead, but the memories are not. Buried, but only as deep as my mind will allow.

I still cry and punch and fight because of him. I am tormented every time the man that I love with all my being touches me in a way. Why cannot he just love me without it feeling wrong? If I smell sweat, stale cigarette smoke, or hear moans of delight and passion, I get cold chills. BUT, at the same time, aroused. Makes absolutely no sense.

If I see someone that I know that at one time or another may have wondered about us, I feel shame and dirty. The one that I know saw us, I feel like it was all my fault. I am not yet a survivor. I am continuously uncovering the past that makes me a victim. He raped me; he raped my soul.

My sister has been my sister since she was born when I was

three. As with many things, I do not remember any of that time. Pictures suggest that we were happy, typical siblings, but now that we are adults, we really were everything but typical.

My earliest memory was when she may have been two or three. We did everything together. We took yummies from the kitchen when nobody was looking. Because she was tiny, she never got in trouble. It was convenient. Not for me, though, I was the good example, good choices girl. We learned how to avoid a bad choices lesson by going to the bathroom in the closet. This was also the period when we got into trouble for asking to go to the bathroom. For me, there was a belt or flyswatter or a freshly peeled switching stick across my lower back and butt. For her, horror and fear as she watched what it was like to set a bad example.

We used to play in the anthills behind our house until the fireflies and mosquitoes came out. Then we went inside our tiny house and took a bath and went to bed. We slept in the same bed until she left when she was sixteen. We have photos of sitting on the stoop together. Still looking quite content.

As we grew a bit older and she caught on to the choice's thing, we butt heads a little, but that's sibling rivalry, right? Once she threw a floor tile at me and hit me in the head. Lots of bleeding, and somehow that was still my fault. I provoked it.

When we were in school, life began to take a turn. I remember that the love from him was not the same for her. Bath time was long, tedious, and uncomfortable. It was also something we never talked about and the one thing that my sister and I did not do together. Sunday was bath night. Sponge baths for the rest of the week. So, to school with dirty greasy hair, come Wednesday, after wearing the same clothes since Sunday, we were very smelly students which invited all sorts of other issues from classmates.

We came home, did homework, ate lunch, and went to bed. Usually, he would come "lay between us until we fell asleep". By five-thirty in the evening, mom was out the door to go to bingo seven nights a week. Usually after begging, borrowing, or yes, stealing her entry into the game.

My sister was not oblivious to the torment that her father was capable of. She often was slapped around for backtalk, but she retaliated and ran away for days on end. She quit school before eighth grade. She met her first boyfriend and hung out with the neighborhood guys, selling nickel bags from the Circle Court Motel. I suffered through additional years of "love" and "torment", graduated high school, started college, and started socializing with girls from school. I had sleepovers and started drinking pink champagne, screwdrivers, keystone light and selling stolen cigarettes from him. I had a few parties in the front yard with beer that he bought. That was the extent of my rebellion.

It was not beneath him to portray himself as an upstanding citizen when we went to JJ Newberry's and were forced to steal things like cigarettes, candy, and food. We took our daily stroll on the weekends and dumpster dives and rifled through garbage for deposit returns. Just one more thing for people to harass us about.

When our lives caused a distance physically, it was one of those things I do not remember. I remember she announced that she had met the love of her life, I remember that she said she was moving away, but I do not remember the day that it happened, and the several months that followed. I just remember that my sister, my person, my friend, was leaving me to fend off the demon that she called her father.

I asked myself on several occasions, why? Why did she not stay at home and finish school, get a job, do what other fifteen-year-old did? It was not until recently that I figured it out. Guilt, denial, anger, sadness. She was dealing with her own set of issues. She is now forty-nine years old. She had a triple bypass three years ago and has COPD. She works eighty hours a week taking care of the elderly, which she seems to love. She has three grown boys. One who has been in jail more than out, one who works like a dog but loves his family like crazy. He is the same that deserves all the happiness in the world. He is a good boy. The youngest, I have always believed to be the "milkman's baby". He and the oldest are firefighters. The youngest is a sweet guy who is also searching for "the one". One day, I hope it finds them.

Her husband is a saint that loves unconditionally. He has spent the last twenty years loving her and treating her like Cinderella. He has forgiven her indiscretions, loving her still. He is truly her Prince Charming.

There were days that I would travel the hour to her house to visit, and she would come to my house with her babies. Then those instances began to get further and further apart. I would call on the telephone and she may or may not answer, but when we did speak, it was good. As time went on, no more calls. When we did speak, there was tension and animosity and we hung up mad at each other.

Now, thirty-two years since she left home, our relationship has plummeted. We last ended with her telling me to have a good life. This was her response to me telling her that I have room only for happiness in my life, and that is what I am looking for. If she cannot contribute to a positive relationship, we need to reevaluate.

I have found that over time, grieving for someone who is still alive is horrifically painful. Where we will be in the days, weeks, or months to come depends on her and what she is looking for in life. I can only hope that one day we could work together to get through it, but time will tell.

My place is very dark, big, very cold, and very cluttered. There are holes in the darkness and then darker holes in the already dark holes. I am wandering aimlessly in this place and on occasion, I drop things in the holes. And then I drop more, and then more, and still more. Guiding me in this process is my friend Sam. I do not know where he was guiding me, or why, I just know that he was helping me make it all ok.

I think that I have come to realize that my long-term memories are in those holes. I do not remember my childhood Christmas, or Thanksgivings, or any birthdays which were ordinary days. I do not remember important things like prom or graduation. Heck, I do not remember my kids growing to where they are today. I feel cheated. They are in the holes, and I can get some of them back. I want to remember them, I prayed all my life for my babies, and I cannot remember them.

It is fourteen days before Christmas, and I am less than excited. I became stressed again. The only reason that I participate is for my babies. They believe. They believe in Santa Claus, and we bake Jesus a birthday cake, it is for them.

I think of Christmas as a time to reflect on family and all the good in life. I am trying hard to change my attitude. My first family has either disowned me or died. My second family, my now first family, shares all the love that they can muster. I am showered with love and gifts and hugs and warmth that I should have been surrounded with before. I cannot help but think of myself as cheated, not gifted. How do I change that?

Until my children were born, I was not a fan of Christmas. I still do not. I love to see the excitement on their faces, the magic of believing. I did believe it once. I believed that if there was a Santa, he would put him on the naughty list, and I would get a real daddy for Christmas.

I did get some nice toys for Christmas. Santa worked hard so that those men could bring us special baskets of toys and food for the holiday. We could have Christmas food, and we could see dolls, and games, and cars, and tractors. But soon after Santa came, they all went away. Mommy said that he needed smoking sticks and mommy needed to go and play cards, so he had to sell all my Christmas stuff.

Who takes a toy from a four-year-old? Dinner was not anything special. Usually, turkey that was too cooked with mashed potatoes and gravy, a little of this and a little of that. All of which were given by charity. By the day after Christmas, any clue that a holiday had just happened was gone.

December twentieth, several years ago, my brother was deemed brain dead. We started the process of having life support withdrawn to allow him peace. It was one of the toughest decisions that we have ever had to make. I say we because Amelia was part of the process. Not because she had to be because I had power of attorney, but because it was right. It was of course, a struggle, only because it was my suggestion, not hers.

On December twenty-seventh, two thousand ten, Robert took his last breath and was granted his forever Christmas wish. I wished him a Merry Christmas as I kissed him and assured him that he would be with Mom again, and for sure, when the time was right, I would join them. I was happy for him but self-ishly sad for me because he was nonjudgmental of anything I had ever done. He was pure by nature and unaltered by others. He never did anything wrong, and I will always believe that he was sent to this earth with a message. I hope that the right person received that message. We enjoyed all our visits, he would smile, and his eyes would shine when I walked into the room. He enjoyed me rubbing his back which nobody else could do. Unfortunately, these visits usually precipitated seizures. I love and miss him.

I am looking forward to the time when I can celebrate the birth of Jesus with my children and reinforce the true meaning.

I was looking through some old journals. Not that I am interested in resurrecting memories of days past, but some things still have not changed since. For example, on November sixteenth, two thousand one, I wrote "work is a joke. Big wig priorities are out of order, and someone does not like the way that I spend my time. Get my head on straight and produce a plan. Easier said than done. I feel like I belong institutionalized. I am going NUTS!!!"

November seventeenth two thousand one - "What a scatter-brain - Nothing makes sense."

January sixteenth two thousand and one - "I had a dream of climbing a mountain of wet grass. Everyone was passing me." I have had this dream several times since. What does this mean?

March twenty-fifth, two thousand and one - "My world is so dark! My family has deserted me. Amelia does not answer the phone. I miss mom, she always came through for me - even if she had no clue.

March seventeenth, two thousand and seven - " I was ready to cry! Margaret, what do I do - Can you help me, etc. Forkas screaming "Bobby" and running for the exits and holding herself hostage outside the door. Jane was pushing chairs and stealing books and soda - going in the bathroom in an isolation toilet, Bernadette sneaking up on people. I started meds at seven-thirty in the evening and just finished at ten-fifteen, just in time to chart and still be late getting home. Geneva is on comfort measures. I am ready to go NUTS! I get so nervous and anxious that I fear that I may say or do something that will hurt someone."

Four twenty-eighth in two thousand and two - "It sounds like mom was a horrible person, and at times, she was - then she suddenly got sick, and I had to come to a personal comfort level that allowed us to be ok when she died which ultimately meant forgiveness. "

August eighteenth two thousand and four - "Just for a fleeting second, as I was driving home, I thought - Would it hurt to drive into the guardrails and keep going - would it be as tough as some of the days that I go through? Yes, it would, because then I wouldn't have Doc and the love that will come eventually."

January twenty-fourth two thousand and four - "I thought that you were over that. What episode are you talking about, the one with Brad? I said no. She is so afraid that I will open an assortment of problems. That the entire world will find out exactly how bad Damian really is. She had to stop the conversation because she did not want to say something that she would regret and that she would have to go to later go to confession for. Again, she doesn't want to deal."

I continue to feel some of these things on occasion, but with different circumstances. It really sucks!

During a recent session with Lisa, she asked me how I felt about the entire reason that brought me to her and Sam in the first place. My response simply put was pissed, mad as hell.

According to Elizabeth Kubler Ross (Kessler, 1969), from what I remember in college, said that there were five stages: Denial and Isolation, Anger, Bargaining, Depression, and then finally Acceptance. I guess, from where I stand, I may never get there. I guess I denied it when my thought process led me to believe that what he was doing was normal for a girl my age, and I was always isolated as I was not allowed to go anywhere.

I am still terribly angry with him for taking what could have been a normal life as a young girl away from me. I did not get to do anything that would allow me to be like my other friends. I was allowed by "John Q Public" to be raped repeatedly without any consequence to him at all. He was a PIG, and a thief. A repeat offender on several levels. He stole my soul, my virginity, and my mind. The selfish BASTARD allowed himself to take my most prized possession and turn it into a chaotic situation. I did not get to decide who the special person would be. Instead, my one and only got sloppy seconds. It was not pleasurable, it hurt like hell. The only thing that got me through was knowing that I was with the only person that I wanted to be with.

The news article regarding his court trial and sentence said that he was to get one day to life for rape, sodomy, and carnal abuse of a child under the age of consent. I know this girl. I know her family, and I celebrate them for calling the police and having him arrested.

"Carnal abuse" was a new term for me. According to the law dictionary, the term that is applied to statutory rape where injury to the female is caused by the attempt to penetrate and have intercourse. AND, according to the crazy-ass urban dictionary, "Gentle-rape. Rape committed without painfully harming or traumatizing the victim, in many cases, is enjoyed by both victim and predator. I could imagine what the defense attorney would say. " I believe, your honor, that my client does not deserve such a harsh sentence as there was no harm done to the victim." "It was a gentle rape." What asshole produced that? Starting May of nineteen sixty-two, he served nine years in Dannemora State Penitentiary, a maximum-security prison and was released in nineteen seventy-one when he married my mother in August of that year. Just in time to do it again, and again, and again.

So, I guess I may always be angry. Pissed. Mad as hell! It is ok because the reason is there.

Discipline was an issue in my house. It depended on how good a girl I had been. In my family, however, I was compliant and terrified of what would happen if I were to disobey either of them. Damian thought of Amelia as a favorite. Probably because she was his child. It was not until recently that I learned that she too was being abused. I certainly felt worthless because Amelia got a lot of attention. She was angry that I was spending more time with him. There certainly was animosity between Amelia and me. In fact, there still is.

Whenever I did what he wanted, I was a good girl, and we got what Amelia and I wanted. If I had my period, or said no, it was like Satan had been released. I, most of the time, was compliant to save anyone any bad repercussions.

I had my first real taste of what a large crowd was about this past weekend when we went to Destination USA - Wonder-Works with my family. We went to the food court and were looking for a seat. As I was looking around for a table, I felt like all eyes were on me. Then, it felt like they were getting up and walking toward me. Matthew was sitting across from me. I stared at him to find some sort of normalcy.

For the remainder of the day, I felt like I needed to be between Matthew and someone else in my family. I could not be the leader or the follower. I needed to be between someone that I knew. I am so very tired that I cannot go out on my own without having these feelings. I just want to have fun with my family, create positive memories and enjoy!

"Give it back to God," Sam said. "He gave it to you, you lived it, give it back." And, that I did. I prayed to the good Lord and said, "I trust that everything that you give to me is a lesson. It is a step on my journey of life." The one thing that hurt me so very much was that I could not feel good about my relationship with my mother. I could not decide if I forgave her or not. I wanted to so badly because deep within me, I knew that she was my provider. My person.

Mom often told me stories of when she was abused by her father. Terribly like how I was abused. She would be so angry when she told me. She would say, "I don't know what to do to help you. Do you think that I want this to happen?". She would tell me that she loved me, and she would give me the momma hug that I yearned for. I loved her, but why? I could not figure out why, in the many years that she knew about it, she could not figure out how to help. She kept saying, "Do you want them to take you away from me." Of course not, but I also did not want to be raped by a madman every day of my life either.

During my conversation with God, I asked him to please help me understand. By some strange miracle and after some time, I did. It was strange. It was like meeting my mother for the first time. In my mind, she is a beautiful, lovable, inspiring woman who carried me throughout the taboo of being out-of-wedlock with grace and without any shadow of doubt looming in her mind that I should not become a physical part of her life.

Mom's face smiles in my mind and I feel warm and safe when I think of her. The glow from her smile lightens my world. I feel her embrace and know that she is with me. I can remember the smell of her rose-scented talc that she used to cover the combination of the stale cigarette smoke and body odor. That was mom, though. That is what I knew, that is what I will always know. I can hear her trying to sing the words to "Old Lang Syne" by Guy Lombardo on New Year's Eve. I can taste her fried pork chops with mashed potatoes and chipped beef gravy. Something that I have not tasted since she passed away in nineteen ninety-five.

2

MY SISTER

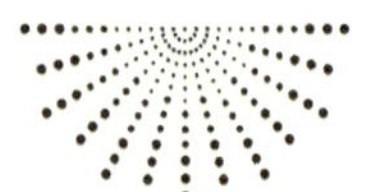

It was late in the evening in mid-April when I checked my phone and noted that I had an email. I checked the email and there it was... My results were in from ancestry.com. Jen and I both went to the computer and called up my email. It told me I was seventy-five percent French, the rest English with a hint of Irish and Scottish. It showed two people who were more than first cousins but not full-blooded siblings. One was Jamie Best, the other Adeline Holman Bova. I wrote to both, stating who I was and my desire to find out who they were to me. The Adeline person wrote back... And scared the shit out of me. She stated she was the result of an extramarital affair and was conceived behind a vault in the local cemetery. This frightened me because I was afraid that this was going to wreck my ideal of my biological family situation. I knew from there that she was a half-sister. The issue was that my biological father and mother were intelligent individuals who would never have sex in a cemetery behind the family vault.

I answered her back, describing my previous life and confessing my sexuality as a lesbian so that if that were an issue for her, she could back out of further contact. She stated that my sexuality was not an issue to her. She confessed to me that she had Multiple Personality

Disorder. I do believe that it is easier for some people to have extreme emotions different from what they think is appropriate and they assign those emotions to other people.

Over the next few months, Autumn and I became closer and were able to prove that each was a sister from the same mister. She told our older brother Thomas of my existence. Thomas was the legitimate son of our father, who fathered half the state of New York. I had another brother who was illegitimate from dad. His name was Tim.

Once it was determined that my biological family was alive, my mother and Jennifer encouraged me to make a trip to New York to meet my biological siblings and mother.

Suddenly this was not some strange story that two people were inventing over email. There she was, a real person with a real husband with my real brother and all of us shared blood and they even looked like me. I gave Autumn the biggest hug imaginable and whispered in her ear a warning I was hoping she would accept and heed. I simply told her "This shit's about to get real"!

This section was written by Paige as I could not put into words what discovering that she was my sister was like. I always needed a big sister; I did not want to be the example for the little sister. I needed guidance and protection. Today, after having known her for the past, almost three things are real. Paige would move mountains for the ones that she loves, and I for her. God really did give me you, and for that, I am forever grateful.

The concept that you oversee your own destiny is not at all new to me. The fact that I have that ability is. All my life, someone else has been in charge, and I was like a puppet following along. Granted, decisions were mine, but usually, they were in the direction of least resistance.

Sending things that I cannot change from my brain, and

heart, back to God is difficult for me. In part because I feel as though I may have failed at some of the tasks. Laying the blame of what happened to me all on everyone else seems somehow not appropriate, yet at the same time, the best thing I could do. Sending something back to God, something that he has already t care of is all I had to do. Accept them.

It is all very easily said, applying them is the difficulty. Letting go of what you have known all your life, and beginning your own journey requires that you take the wheel and weather the storm.

In my life I have seen myself as a victim of many things – trauma, incest, sodomy, beatings, verbal abuse, and a mugging. This was not only by my stepfather, but my uncle, my father, and a neighbor who I thought I knew. There have been so many things that have felt out of my control.

My sense of myself as powerless, violated, and vulnerable runs through the themes of my voices and me, for the lack of a better term, "crazy". The "frozen" child, the inquisitive child, the warden, and the "enforcer" – a stable yet protective force and presence that came from within me – threatening to take over my body (the ultimate in powerlessness). The belief I had in being part of a government process effectively prevented me from believing that others would be able to help (compounding the helplessness I already felt).

I am my own worst enemy, I am bound by my own thoughts. I am still waiting for my ransom to be paid. I forget most of what happens in parts of my day. I remember nothing some-times. It is more than what the average brain can reference as forgetfulness. I did not forget; I just do not remember. I do not remember the ride home. I do not remember tucking the kids in, which totally fucking sucks!!!

If you see crazy as carrying messages relating to an individ-ual's life story and the way they feel about it, my crazy screams VICTIM. Still, the deeper the craziness took me, the more powerless I became. I lost friends, family, my independence and

– at times – my freedom. The more powerless I become, the deeper I fall into insanity. It is a cycle that seems impossible to break.

Once the medication had helped to squash some of my experiences, to deaden the sadness just a bit, the powerlessness remained. I felt unable to take control of my life and – believing myself to be 'crazy' I felt lost. I saw my own value of life on a good day and the medication as being the only thing standing between me and complete madness. The idea of myself as part of the solution just does not compute.

If I look at myself as more a survivor rather than a victim, I have a completely different take on events. My vision is blurred, still by the faces that created this need to question myself as a person. The voices, nightmares and flashbacks still hovering over me like a storm cloud waiting to let loose. Seconds, minutes, even hours remain unaccounted for regularly. I squint to see any light that could be called encouraging. In time, I am told that I will see them as a creative way of coping with experiences that would have otherwise overwhelmed me, or worse. They are a strategy that I can look forward to being capable of and proud of, rather than a problem or flaw.

As a survivor, I hope to have the opportunity to recognize the impact of my life experiences without being a victim. I would like to be able to hold on to the reality of what I have been through while recognizing that this is in the past. Those who have hurt me will have no power except that which I give them.

As a survivor, I will steer my own boat through the calm seas of my new life and my history. I will write my own narrative rather than letting other people create it. It is my life; I am the one who must live it.

Making the transition between victim and survivor is not easy for me. Entering the mental health system when at my most vulnerable compounded this. My journey began thirty years ago and while trying to find solitude amidst the battle that still exists in my mind, I was given a technical-sounding theory that explained why it was that I was flawed – Anxiety, depression, PTSD, all of which are "illnesses". It is such an appealing theory that moving beyond it has been slow and, at times, painful.

If I see my mind as flawed, if I see his face, smell his sweat, and feel his hands around my throat, it is hard to truly take control of my life and see myself as anything other than a victim. I am slowly inching forward but still, I see the victim more than a survivor. In seeing the vision of what I want for my children and from what I envision the other half of my adult life as being, I am starting to feel obliged to try.

In the end, it will have been a process of putting each piece of the puzzle together, standing back and letting myself see what I have created.

I always said that I would not change anything that has happened in my life for anything. I hold strong with that statement. If I had declined one offer, or changed one step, or made one different decision, I might not have been where I am now. I would not be able to learn from a traumatic childhood, or comfort my children, or know what true love was like.

Changing my traumatic past may have been beneficial, but at the same time would not have encouraged me to find out what it is to have personal strength and fortitude. I would not know what courage to be an individual and willingness to thrive was like.

I am often asked, "how did you do it"? I do not know how, but I am happy I did.

I am not angry anymore with her. I am blessed to have had her in my life for the twenty-five years that I did. She taught me lessons that I did not know that I was learning. I can only hope that as she looks down on me from wherever Heaven is, she can feel proud of the person that I am becoming. I hope she feels happy about her grandchildren that I am raising and the choice to break the link of abuse and to be heard. I met my mother today. I cannot wait to get to know her better.

The black shadow that continues to lurk in my psyche decided that he wanted to speak to me this week. According to him, I am a pig, a poor mother, a bad housekeeper, a sinner in many ways. The sinner part I am not one hundred percent sure of, but I am sure that his talking trash needs to be confronted. I would be lying, though, if I did not admit that I was a bit scared of doing so. Fear is a part of what I believed to be a spot of paranoia at times recently. Matthew, at some point in our lives, will hurt me. That cannot be further from the truth. One day I will kiss my baby's goodbye for the day at school and I will never see them again. Fear for any mother. At that point, with Sam, I began to cry. A very raw emotion that I hate doing in public. For me crying is a sign of weakness.

Life has a track record for proving these fears false. Sam says that I need to remember this. He further states that I should get the message from the dark shadow and if he decides not to help with providing information that I should tell him to get out of my life. I have a bigger purpose, and his existence is not needed or wanted.

We were privileged to see Brandon for a reading. Brandon hit the spot on. He said that my brother and mother were present. Robert was saying that he is no longer struggling and that his energy lives in my son, Noah. He can run, and laugh, and play like he was never able to in his journey on earth. Robert further said that he is thankful for me being his Angel on earth. Brandon said that my mother shunned Robert and me. There is not another person on earth that knows this story except for Amelia. And Amelia does not believe in mediums.

Robert was admitted to Sunmount State School for the mentally retarded. Hearsay would have it that the staff there were less than compassionate. They believed heavily in medication to the point of being catatonic. Physically, the residents were abused. The bruises were covered with statements like, "you know how they are". He remained there until the late eighties when he was transferred to Essex County ARC, where he was placed in an IRA in Schroon Lake. The option of someplace closer was present, but mom did not want to be tempted to see him. Mom never saw Robert from the time he was admitted to Sunmount until the day she died in Nineteen ninety-five.

We were being shunned by my mother. The shun was twofold. Once for Robert and once for me. It was the blatant disregard to helping me after I told her that I was being raped by her husband. There was some validation and closure to this three and a half-minute message from the other side.

Saying goodbye to Damian was the best thing that I had ever done in my life. Could that be the end that is referenced in the dream?

I have been working hard for a new beginning. I have been decluttering the pantry in my mind of the old with the intention of bringing fresh, vibrant, and invigorating new to the space.

Some days I feel like I am one of those little ships trapped in a bottle floating in the sea, with the possibility of never being found. Some days I feel like I am stuck in the realm of my own brain, not able to get out without being followed by another version of myself.

Although some days it is comforting to feel like I am not alone, others, I would love to be. Solitude, I understand, is something that is nurturing to the soul and quite helpful to the mind.

I know that my solitude is not something that I can really control on an average day. Uniting the "society" is something that I need to encourage and work for.

Rikki is still standing guard against the secrets that she holds in the back of my mind. Mae sits watching everything that happens daily. She never says a word, but her presence is well-known. Betsy is the nurturer who waves everything off as coincidence and comforts you with her split tongue. I wonder if she really wants to get involved. Emmy is still screaming like a child just finding her voice. She laughs loud, cries loud and never makes any sense at all. Lilly is a slightly older version of Emmy, only she speaks words of experience. She loves to run in the yard while holding Emmy's hand. She loves to smell the tulips and lilacs, watch the birds, and go out with the dog. She now is never alone, she is taking Emmy and showing her the way.

My days are filled with questions being answered in my mind by sometimes other versions of myself. Sometimes I wonder what it would have been like just to never know.

I love to run, or at least I used to. I ran cross-country and track in school. I ran streets when I graduated, I run on the treadmill now at the cardiology office. Did you see that age thing happening, huh? I am no longer able to run because the aches in my knees have gotten the better of me.

This afternoon, I went to see Lisa. In my rearview mirror, it appeared again and again, nobody there. Nothing is said, I feel nothing but uneasy. Of course. There is just another figment of my imagination that makes me feel crazy.

My dream brought all the good feelings back as I continued running down the road. A road that I am not familiar with but like. I think. The cool air hitting me in the face, the even panting in my breath, the burn in my legs. It "hurt so good".

In the distance, I see that I am not alone in my journey down this unfamiliar road. Someone else is also enjoying it. The form, the height, weight, the ponytail, they all look like mine. Like I am chasing myself. I can feel my speed increase. My breathing becomes labored, I get the wrench in my side from lactic acidosis. I want to slow down, but I also want to see who this person is.

I run and run faster and faster still, but she is still too far to catch. One of these days, I will.

One of the most confusing things is how our bodies respond during the abuse. How can something that feels scary, wrong, and shameful also feel so good? Often a strategic pedophile grooms his or her victims by awakening their sexual desire, making them a more willing, compliant partaker in how our bodies respond during the abuse. How can something that feels terrifying, immoral, and disgraceful also feel so good? I can remember feeling pleasure while being abused. More confusion about why it was wrong.

3

EMME AND LILY

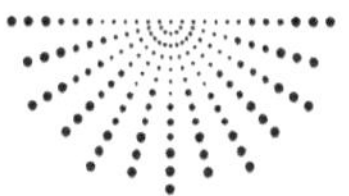

During one of my sessions with Sam, I discovered that I was not living this life alone. I was living it with two little girls. Their names were Emme and Lily. Emme seemed shy, scared, dirty, malnourished… abused. She comes to mind peeking around a wall or a large piece of furniture. I later realized that that little girl was me. She was the me that lived in the days of torment with Damian and Mom. She was the little girl that disconnected herself from my life and went into hiding while I went on seeing the world in unusual ways.

I really want them to share my world, to let them know that there is love and decency. My task is to figure out how to get them to join me. What are they afraid of? How can we alleviate that fear? Is there anything that they need help with. It all remains to be seen. As time rolled on, Emme's counterpart, Lily, surfaced.

Emme loves life. She is very inquisitive, wanting to know why the grass is green, why the birds do not speak, how does she catch the butterfly. She often speaks for Lily, teaching her the way that life could really be. She is never afraid and embraces every moment of every day. Loves the playground, the toy aisle at Target, and seeing animals for the first time. She plays with Jeter, our family dog, and talks to him.

Lily is an adorable, beautiful little girl who wants to play. She is giggling, from the toe's kind of giggle. She is about four or five, I see her peeking a lot. Of late, she has come from around the corner that she was peeking from and is standing, I think, in front of something. I never see Lily below the waist. Even when we played in leaves, she was buried from the waist down. Today, it felt like Lily saw her first snow. She wanted to play. I slipped in slush, and she thought it was fun. Really quite frightening for me, but she loved it. I smile. Lily is often referring to herself as a bad girl because that is what she was told for most of her life by "daddy". Her friend Sam shed some new light on the scenario by offering that Lily wanted a "daddy". I wanted a dad. Until I met Matthew and his dad, I never knew what one truly was. I loved him so very much because he treated me like a daughter. A real daughter, not a sex slave. I could talk to him about everything. Not a single thing that I told him was misinterpreted, rather, it was listened to and supported. I could hug him and feel warmth and family. I never had to guess. Now he is gone. Fatherless again.

In my second session with Sam, I had another trance and the little girl reached out to me with her arm. I tried but could not reach her. She touched me, but I could not feel her. This time, the goal of the trance was to eradicate the fear, anger, and hatred that was inside me. Figuring it out, though, was the problem. If there was a course of events that could be changed, how could I change it? I still do not know. That night I saw the faces of Brad, Thomas, Victor, and Damian. One of them was stabbed. I do not know which one.

Emme hears rough voices, threatening voices, bad man voices. She sees decayed teeth that are never brushed, that are yellow and fake. Short stubby hairs on a dark ruddy face with bushy eyebrows that look like one. Eyeglasses that do not cover the cold demonic eyes that rape her at every glance. She smells the old cigarette smoke coming from his breath that seems to get faster and faster. The only thing that she cannot do is feel him as he breaks her tiny little toes with his bare hands, and dislocated fingers by pulling them out of joints. She cannot scream because he is crushing her. She cannot run, she cannot feel. She wants it all to go away. Lilly is her outlet. Lilly is her person. Lilly is how she trusts.

The question should not be how I get to trust, it should be why I should trust. Life has not shown its ugly head in a way that you get it, until you lose it. I trust the people that I am supposed to and where did that get me?

In another session with Sam, I had another trance and again, Emme reached out to me with her arm. I tried but could not reach her. She touched me, but I could not feel her. If there was a course of events that could be changed, how could I change it? I still do not know.

Babies, in general, symbolize something in your own inner nature that is pure, vulnerable, helpless and/or uncorrupted. Emme and Lily are those vulnerable little delicate flowers that need nurturing. Emme needs Lily to thrive and vice versa. Lily has helped Emme find her screech voice, now continues to help with her inner voice that can giggle, laugh, and sing. Emme wants to chase butterflies and is curious about caterpillars. She wants to skip around the yard and swing on a tire swing with her golden locks of hair flowing in the breeze. Just not yet. Lily is still her person. She still needs help. Emme has stories to tell that only Lily can hear. Mom and I shared what was love before Damian came. I slept with her each night. I remember walking with her down the street. I saw lots of things. Of course, I am in a stroller, but people smiled at me. Or were they laughing at me? I was wearing the same clothes that I did a week ago, and I do not remember my last bath. My hair is a mess. We went to grandma's house. We saw Uncle Ricky and Aunt Janice. Uncle Ricky picked me up and sat me on his lap and we played. It was fun. He smelled funny. He smelled like smoking sticks. He did that a lot. Grandma was making some white gravy, which was my favorite. She likes them with mashed potatoes and pork chops.

Uncle Ricky gave us a ride home because it was dark. I was washed up with a dirty washcloth that was used for everything else. It was stinky. Mom tucked me in and climbed in next to me. I was happy, and she was too.

I do not remember when my step monster came, just that he was not there, then he was. I did not get to sleep with mom anymore. It was all him. A small-time later, they got married. Not all fancy like a wedding party should be. They went on some trip after. I spent time with Aunt Freda and Uncle Orlie. My house was not fun anymore. I do not like sharing it with this man.

All my stuff went away. My bed went to someone else for money. I did not have toys except for a giraffe. We did everything together. He was as tall as Uncle Sam.

That man said "you ain't all that good anyway, just a tasty ripe little tight peacha ass. Just a new pussy. I made you what you are. You ungrateful little bitch!"

"Remember, you made it up, or you die! your choice."

What was my choice? He did not ask! He just did dreadful things to me and then it was my fault. What is he talking about? What is a "peacha ass"? And we do not have a kitty. I am not a bitch; I am a big girl. He is confused.

My thoughts are that I can do something now that I could not do then. I can better protect them from the predators, I can keep her happy and healthy, clean, and warm. I can fight for her. Nobody can take her things away. I can give her things. I will always love her, even if she does or says something that is not right, I may be disappointed, but I will tell her right. I can find time for fun and play. I will continue to encourage her to come back to my life. I will share with her the happiness that I feel.

My name is Lily, Emme is my *bestest* friend. We see a man that was in jail for being not nice to a girl once. He came to our mom when he came home and then she had a wedding with him. Momma says that he will never go away because he is hers and she is his. How can one person own another one? I am so confused.

He sucks on some stinky smoking sticks that cost a lot of money. He does it a lot. Momma says that I cannot have my bed anymore because he sold it to get more smoking sticks. We do not have food because he needs his smoking sticks. The lights do not come on at night because he needs his smoking sticks.

Mom says that the hot water heater is broken because he needs smoking sticks, and he drank too much last night. Momma is mad and puts some hot stinky stuff in his underwear so that his peepee will get burned. Momma thinks that it is funny, but it hurts me because he will hit me. He will think that I did it and not momma. He will not believe me when I say no, I was right.

Momma took money from his pocketbook to go to BINGO. He knew. He always counts his money. He got mad and momma cried. Momma cries a lot because she cannot go because she has no money until the welfare check comes on the third of the month.

The third is here and momma and he got big *samiches* from Ti Pi. They look so good. I would like ham. We do not get to have any because I have been bad. I do not know what I did, but I am bad. I get to have some beans in a can. They are not too bad. Tomorrow, mom and he are getting a pie with tomatoes, cheese and *roni's* on it. I hope I get to have some. I did not.

I heard something in momma's bedroom that sounded like momma might be crying. I sneaked out of my door and peeked. The light was still on, so I could see everything. I do not think he was hurting her. She was hugging him so very tight. She was moaning like she was in pain, but I do not think that she was. He was on top of her and pushing up and down. He or momma had no clothes on. I do not like that game. His bog thing was out. He was pushing faster and faster and faster. Then, he climbed down and went to bed.

I heard that sound again from momma. I peeked again and he had his face in momma's momma parts. Mom screamed "Oh God." I prayed that momma would be ok. Now I know what to do the next time he does that to me. I cannot help but think that this happens a lot. Why does it not feel good when he does that to me. I do not know how it feels. I cannot feel anything.

I keep watching because I want to be sure. I want to be sure that I am doing the right thing, when it is my turn again. I need to be like Momma and pray, so that good things happen to me. He says though that I cannot tell Momma what a good girl I am. I am sure Momma would be proud.

My turn came very soon. This time, I had to go downstairs, where it was stinky, dark, and cold. I must lay on the cold floor and do just as he says. I took my pants off. I took off my undies like Momma did. I am a good girl. This time he made me touch his boy parts with my hands. It felt funny, like slime. It was gritty, like there was some dirt in it. YUCK! I am not happy about that. I told him that I did not like how it feels. He hit me in the mouth. My lip was bloody. He put his boy thing in me and then spit on his hand and rubbed my poop hole. He put something cold in it. I remember lots of blood and boo boos. I still cannot feel anything. I looked after, and it was the handle part of a hammer.

I made a mistake and told Momma what happened. I told her what a good girl I thought I was. She asked about my lip and the cut. I told her that I told him that I did not like to touch his big boy thing. She told me not to lie because it is bad. I am a bad girl.

I am Emme's person. I was four when daddy hit me. He hit me because I cried cuz he gave me boo boos in my butt. He said that big girls enjoy that. I do not like that because it hurts. I have big boo boos because I bleed a lot. Mommas say that I have big poop, which is why I bleed. I am a bad girl because I am not a big girl.

I love everything about this life. I ask a lot of questions. I want to know why the grass is green, why the birds tweet instead of talking like every other people. How do I catch a butterfly? I help Lily see how this world is supposed to be. I am not afraid and hang on to every moment of every day. We both play with Jeter and talk to him.

Momma, he hurt me, he is always hurting me. He told me not to tell a lie. I cannot keep this secret anymore. It feels like I am not telling the truth. I feel like I did it and I am bad. This secret is wrong because he hurt me. He made me bleed. He said that no one wanted a virgin, I asked Momma. She said "It is someone that has never had *innercuss*."

What is *innercuss*, Momma? She said that I would learn about it in school. But I am four. He said that I am not so innocent anymore, because he took it. I am still a virgin, but not pure. That is what he said. I love him, but daddy love. He said, "it's like Momma love." You are my momma. He told me not to tell. Daddy said that he was making me ready for the boy that would love me like Daddy loves Momma when they have a married party.

His hand touched my skin over my heart. His hand was rough, bumpy, like Momma says happens with arduous work and shaking like he was excited. I was shivering, but I was not cold.

He squeezed and sucked on my boobies like a lollipop. It felt weird. His hand was moving around my body like he was checking for chickenpox, until he reached my important spot. I cried because I was scared. He covered my face with his hands, pulled my legs apart and he put his fingers inside me. I tried to scream for Momma, but I could not. I was bleeding when I went to the potty. I was a bad girl.

I do not like to be home. Amelia knows but does not tell because he does special things for her at my expense. "Daddy, don't make me ride Autumn naked around the house." "Daddy, can I have a ...." Of course, he gave it to her.

He locks my door from the outside so that I cannot run away. I can hear the keys and know what he wants from me. He comes over, rips off the sheets, and unzips his pants. I plead, "Daddy, please don't, it hurts very badly." I try to scream, and he covers my mouth. He looks at me and, with his breathless voice, asks,"does it feel good?" I look at him, not really seeing him and shake my head yes. I really did not feel a thing. I am numb.

He pushes me faster and faster until his head goes up in the air, he gets a smile on his face, and he makes me all messy. Just when he is done, he pushes me onto my knees, pulls up my nightie and puts his special thing into my butt. He pees and then tells me to go to the bathroom, he laughs at me the entire way.

The first time he touched me, I was shy and just wanted mommy. I was nervous, but he said that every daddy does it. Do not be afraid. Why did nobody tell me this, why did mommy not tell me this was going to happen. Is it supposed to be a major surprise? Everybody must keep it a secret.

His hands were rough, bumpy, like mommy says happens with challenging work and shaking like he was excited. I was shivering like I was cold, but I was not.

He told me no one wanted a virgin, what is a virgin, I asked mommy. She said that it is someone that has never had *innercuss*. What is *innercuss*, mommy. She said that I would learn about that in school. But I am four.

Daddy said that he was making me ready for the boy that would love me like daddy loves mommy when they have a married party.

His hand touched my skin over my heart. He squeezed and sucked on them like a lollipop. It felt weird. His hand was moving around my body like he was checking for chickenpox, until he reached my important spot. I cried because I was scared. He covered my face with his hand and told me to not make any noise because mommy would get mad at me. His rough hands pulled my legs apart and he put his fingers inside me. I tried to scream for mommy, but I could not. I was bleeding when I went potty. I was a bad girl.

Momma, why are you so sad? But I am not lying, Momma, Momma, please do not be sad. I just want it to stop. Momma, why are you mad at me, I am a bad girl, I knew it. He does terrible things to me when you go to Bingo. He touches my special thing when you are watching tv. He makes me go for walks with him. He makes me go into the bushes and lay in the grass. I do not want to do it anymore. I must go downstairs to the basement. I do not like it there. If I am quiet and a good girl, we get treats. We can have some bread, or go for a walk, or watch some tv. But Momma, I am not telling a lie!

One time when he got done with my special spot, he had a grin on his face, and he made me all messy. Just when I think I can go to bed, he pushes on my knees, he pulls up my nightie and puts his special thing in my butt. He pees and then tells me to go to the bathroom, he laughs at me the entire way.

I remember the first time he touched me, I was shy and just wanted Momma. I was a lot nervous, but he said that every daddy does it. Do not be afraid. Why did nobody tell me this? Why did Momma not tell me this was going to happen. It is supposed to be a major surprise. Everybody must keep it a secret.

That man said that mommy was dead. He said that she died. Why am I so sad? Why did I still love her when she did not believe me? Why do I still love when she said that I was a bad girl? I do not understand. Mommy would never just leave. She would not leave me with this person who does all the bad.

4

MAE

ae is ten years old and in the fifth grade. This was a tough class of kids because they would say terrible things about me. Things like you smell or I like the spaceships on your sneakers. On the bus, Rhonda and a bunch of other girls made me bring down my pants to check if I had clean pants on. I really wanted to quit school.

I had a thought that would take care of all of it. I went into my mother's bedroom and looked at her medications. She took a lot of them. I needed something that could do the worst damage. I found the bottle with the pills in it that fixed Momma's nerves when she was not well in her head. She only had ten lefts. At that moment, mom asked what I was doing. I told her that I had a headache and needed some medicine. She handed me some Tylenol and told me that the next time, I just needed to ask. I needed to figure something else out.

This morning, I woke up to a voice yelling at me AUTUMN!!!! I was startled and awoke, shaking and unable to function for a moment. I do not think I was dreaming because Matthew had just asked me to help him put on his compression, so I knew that she was there, on watch, but she never said anything. Sam also clarified her purpose because when I first met Mae, she would wake me up in the middle of the night by yelling my name. She is the first protector. She tells me that only terrible things happen in the dark. At one point in my life, she was so right, now she understands that she is ok to allow me to sleep. Mae also never moves. She sits there. Nothing below the waist, like Lily, waiting and watching.

I cannot really see her anymore. I know that she is there because I see a sheet of paper with the word "DIE" handwritten on it. Who does she want to die? Her, me, him? I just do not know. I am a bit scared, but I do not know of what. Am I just making things bigger than they really are? We shall see.

My daddy is scary, I told JoJo, who is my BFF and next-door neighbor all through school. We could tell each other everything. He often hurts me, I told her. She had a look of disbelief on her face. I told her Momma, Margaret too. She told me to tell mommy. I did, but she does not believe me. I told Mr. Timmins, he was the therapy, social worker at school, and nothing happened.

5

BETSY

etsy is the grandma. The grandma that I went to when I was sad and needed a super hug. She was awesome. She is my voice of reason. She sits in the foreground, quietly and consoling sole who speaks only the truth about everything. Gram is waiting for me to make a bad choice. She does make sense. She reminds me of my grandmother. Gram was a witty older woman who had something to say for everything. No filters and no ifs, ands, or buts. She would love for all her kids and grandkids to be under one roof. When Betsy is around, I feel comforted. There is warmth and happiness.

I met Betsy a few days ago. She is a quiet and consoling sole who speaks only truth about everything. Nothing is sugarcoated. She is the person to tell you when you are wrong and when you are right. Betsy is like my grandmother. When Betsy is around, I am comforted. There is warmth and happiness. My "Betsy" was toothless, with usually a cigarette or cigar hanging from her mouth. It never felt bizarre to see. It would be questionable if we never got to see it. She was always doing something for her family. Cooking, sewing, cleaning, making butter, etc. Something for everyone else, and never herself.

Betsy came to me during one of my sessions with Sam. It seems as if she wanted to clarify some information that I only assumed was true based on what I am told. When I was in elementary school, now considered grade school, I had a mishap on the playground. While on the teeter-totter, I fell backwards, was left unconscious and needed to have some stitches. Well, according to Betsy, truth be known, I had a mishap in the basement while being raped where my head was hit against the wall and I was unconscious. I had to go to the emergency room and get twenty-seven stitches.

Why did they believe them, why did they not question why a school representative was not there with me? Still, once again, failed by the system.

During her final years on earth, she told me that I was an old soul, that I had been where she was going, but came back because I had a bigger purpose. I believed her. A part of my soul died the day that she left this journey in life for the next.

6

RIKKI

ikki is another alter. She appeared near the beginning of my diagnosis of DID (dissociative identity disorder). At first, I was not sure of Rikki's gender because she was such a strong and protective force. She dressed like a "tomboy" with flannels, overalls, long greasy hair, and work boots. If she came from my psyche, I wondered where. I was initially agitated with her because that was not the person that I had become. I was quiet, isolated, and timid. I backed down from confrontation. I did not like her until I understood her.

Rikki, she is protector number two, a bit different from Mae in that Rikki feels that she needs to protect me from everyone. She is a tough cookie to negotiate with. She hates men. All men. She thinks of Sam as her nemesis. She is vulgar, dominating, and I think misunderstood. I am still trying to figure her out. Not in a bad sense, I just do not know what she wants me to do.

So, this crazy Bitch is at it again. She is so fucked up it is not even funny anymore. Today, she cries, she sees herself from another perspective. The first place she runs to is to see Sam or

Mirko, or whoever the fuck he is. He gives this crazy bitch what she is lacking. I do not get it. Then again, I do not have to.

Today she is in self-destruct mode. Over the top. Not many have seen the craziness like today. Had to be on my toes with her today. Driving was a bit hairy; walking was scary even for me. Stagger and sway. I cannot think of another time since I have been saving her pitiful ass where I thought things could go that wrong. But again, Rikki saved her sorry fucking ass again.

So, in honor of my nemesis, Sam, or Mirko! HOLY FUCK, FUCK, FUCK!!! I cannot wait to see how you are going to fix this friggin' mess.

I am the badass of this little "society." Autumn and I have finally come to understand and admire each other. I shed some light on my position as her protector during my last session with "Sam."

Who is the one who put their hands over your quivering fucking mouth so that you did not get the snot punched out of you? Who is the one who made you blackout so that you did not scream when you nearly bled to death giving birth to a dead baby? Who is the one who got you through wiping up your bloody crotch the first time? Who stopped you from killing yourself not once or twice, but four times? It was me! If it were not for me! You would be dead! DEAD!!!

You are fucking crazy waste of space WAKE UP! You are such a pansy-ass that you cannot make decisions for yourself. You would much rather make other people happy than be happy yourself. You are the pathetic bitch that you are because you never listened to me. I told you to go to the cops, but you did not. And, what happened? You got raped again, repeatedly.

Your friend is so fucked up if he thinks the war is over. This war is far from over. It has consumed you. Your everyday is this war! Let it go! I still fight for you! Tell your fucking lazy assed husband to take out the garbage and mow the lawn. You do not need to be doing that and the June Cleaver shit that you do already. Say NO when you want to! Say FUCK OFF when you should. Your friend was right when he said that. Do not bottle up the hostility, say what you feel. I still must fight, because you cannot, or is it do not?

The war is not over. I am not talking to him until he can honestly convince me otherwise. Then, and only then, do we have something to discuss.

During this attack in Nineteen eighty-five, is when we guessed that Rikki manifested and became a very real personality in my life. Rikki shared with me that when I was raped, I also conceived a child. This session has changed my life forever. In general, that all the information that I know. I do know that through this session that the baby did not survive.

Autumn was not able to comprehend that she was a mother at the age of fifteen. She had so many questions that I was not able to answer. Her questions were doused with sadness. She wanted to know where her baby was, boy or girl? Her faith taught her that she should not question why because it was part of a master plan. She does occasionally question her faith like this and prays that God will provide the answers.

How am I supposed to wrap my head around the idea that I was a mother at the age of fifteen? So many questions are coming into my head. Although extreme sadness is dousing those questions, I cannot get past the one question. Where is my baby? A mother needs to know where her babies are. Alive or not. Was my baby a boy or a girl? I try not to question why, because I passionately believe that it was all in God's master plan. I do, however, on occasion question my faith at times like this and pray that God will provide the answers.

I am in a dark place right now and have been very selective about who I choose to talk to about this situation. My husband and his mother are the only two people in this world that I have said anything to outside of "Sam". I tried to talk to Matthew last night. I am in disbelief at what he had to say. Of course, Matthew is often struck with not having the right words when it comes to tragedy. I was told that I dwelled on it too much over the weekend. That I mentioned it to him on many occasions when I should have been focused on something else. During one of those times, I was holding a two-week-old infant. He told me that I am not the only one that has ever been in this situation. A lot of people have become pregnant because of rape. As far as he needs to know, dwelling is done because I will not speak to him about it again. Meaning no offense, but unless you have carried a child near your heart for any amount of time or because the child was not yours does not negate the fact that the child existed.

Rikki took me by the hand as she led me to the little shed that once was a playhouse for my sister and me. It then was turned into a chicken coop. I hated those chickens. They attacked anything and everything that came around them.

Much to my dismay, Rikki led me inside and told me to investigate the corner of the coop under the nests where the hens lay their eggs. I can only imagine what they will do once I disrupt their living space.

Once moving the shelf that housed the nests, I moved a piece of wood that revealed some black plastic. Removing some of the earth from the bag, the feeling that came over me was indescribable. I felt intense sadness and shivers. I knew that that was my son. Rikki took my hand and brought me out of the hen house and into the main house where years of torment had happened. Why do I need to come back when I had vowed years ago, that I would never? I began to feel the hate all over again.

She led me to the basement door, where I stopped instantly and did not want to go. This is a very dark and cold place that produced nothing but pain and bad memories. With Mirko's help, he encouraged me to go with Rikki. She will not let anything hurt me. She manifested when I was brutally tortured and left for dead. I made it to the bottom of the stairs. I look around, and nothing has changed. The fuel tank is still at the foot of the stairs, and the hot water heater that continuously leaked was right next to it. There were two rooms. Each was dark, damp, and musty with cobwebs, spiders, and mice occupying each.

To the immediate right, there was the room. The room with the mattress on the floor where all the incest took place, where a lot of the secrets were hidden. I see myself lying on the mattress in agony. My underwear was off, and I had my knees to the side. He was at the foot of the mattress with a bunch of crap all around him. He was yelling at me to stop screaming. I could not. The pain was so intense. He was pulling on something from between my legs. I screamed again, and he hit me. This time everything went black.

I woke up to feel as though I had been murdered and was looking at a crime scene. There was blood all around me. The mattress was saturated, and the blood was dripping off the edge onto the floor. I looked down and he was cutting an umbilical cord with a rusty hatchet. I had had a baby.

From what I could tell, he was fully developed, a boy, weighed about two pounds. He was not breathing, and he was doing nothing to help him. He threw him into a black garbage bag and tied it up. He told me to clean myself up and locked the basement door. He came back a brief time later and told me that mom was coming home. He said nothing happened. I was to tell nobody. I would die.

He dragged me up the bathroom stairs and pushed me into the bathroom, where I took a quick sponge bath with a washcloth and soap. He came in and raped me again. He was yelling at me, saying that that baby should have been his. I cheated. I was a slut. I am a dirty whore.

I told Rikki that I wanted to come back, and Mirko helped me reorient myself to my safe place. To the place where all my ghosts come out. At that point, I really wished that he were still alive. So that I could kill him. I was reminded that if I did that, I would not see my babies and would not be able to spend my happily ever after with Matthew. I can only hope that he is where he belongs alongside the devil beneath the depths of hell.

7

LADY MAYBELLINE

I am the seventh wonder of Autumn's world. Even today, I must ask her "why would you wear something like this to a party?" "I like this dress," she would respond. "It is comfortable, sensible, and non-wrinkling after washing." Sensible is nice, but so is elegance and style. You are a fifty-year-old woman. Act your age, you have not an ounce of masculinity in you.

"I bet I could find a good dose." Autumn replied. "I can change the oil in my car like the best. I can change the filter in a furnace, I can wear an awesome pair of work boots just like the rest." But you can also wear a sensible haircut, a bit of makeup, and a beautiful outfit too, only if you let yourself. "I enjoy comfort." But don't you like compliments for you being you? "Yes, but I really do not like the attention. I left in disgust. Victory for Autumn, this time.

Lady Maybelline was in the same class as Autumn. One day, she brought Autumn a few of her clothes. Lady was tiny but strong. She had red hair and dressed nicely. She brought Autumn a pair of Dockers with a nice pink plaid blouse that would look nice for any day of school and even prevent her from taking crap from anyone about her appearance.

8

AMANDA

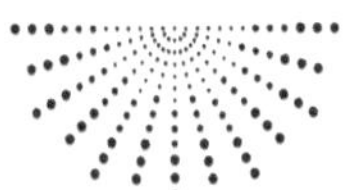

So now we know that the theory that women of abuse often become gay. I so see it. I, at some point, had the idea that I was gay. There were some relationships that teetered online with being a lesbian. Bisexual, because men and I also have had relationships that would indicate that I was not gay. Jeannie was a woman that I once shared an apartment with. She tried subtly to make advances toward me. When I was asleep, I would find her running her hands up and down my breastbone uttering unintelligible whispers that made me quiver while I pretended to sleep.

Jeannie later went to live with another woman and had a lesbian affair until her lover moved away and got married. Jeannie and I have since grown apart as time and distance often bring about.

I often find myself looking in the direction of a beautiful woman. Usually checking out one of her attributes. I guess it does not say that I am gay if I check them out, it's only if I act on them.

I do not like it when Autumn sleeps with her husband. Selfish, I know, but why is a tradition that a man and woman must love one another. She just is not down with the whole idea, but a bit of her may. I know that Autumn sometimes notices that Matthew does not pay obvious attention to other women. Autumn points out when a woman is not wearing panties or a bra. Matthew asking how she would know such things. Autumn assures him that all she needs to do is pay attention.

A beautiful woman is a monument of true class and elegance. Beautiful being stressed. Not an attempt to be beautiful with the ultimate result being trashy. It is an art form.

One day I was eating salty food, chips, or something similar. My tongue began to be very painful. This pain took me back to a memory when mom wanted to cut my tongue off for calling her a son of a bitch. Thank goodness that she had poor knife skills as she did cut me, but I still have my tongue. Interestingly enough, there is a scar on the right side of my tongue that would suggest that there was at one time some trauma.

At the end of the day, and after a lifetime of counseling, my "society" will integrate into this one amazing mind that will remember the trauma that I endured, but will allow me the discretion of dealing on my own with the flashbacks that are long gone memories that I need not worry about, since I have been groomed substantially with an amazing "Sam". Although this conquest may take forever, the pain and dissociation of everyday life will be long behind me and although the pain may still be there, it will be phantom pain because it was relocated and worked through. I will be able to live a normal, whatever that is, happy and undisturbed life.

Although my little group of alters will still be with me, they will be integrated into this circle of friends that will be with me wherever I go. Emme and Lily will run with the butterflies and swing in the wind. Mae will continue to look at the children. Rikki will always be my enforcer and keep me safe. Amanda will be ok with my sexuality and enjoy looking through my eyes at the occasional woman with class. Betsy will forever be in my memory as the woman who loved me unconditionally and kept me on the straight and narrow. Collectively, they will be the me that survived the many years of torment, until someone started to listen.

END

ACKNOWLEDGEMENT

There are a few people that I need to thank as there are a few folks that I have talked about my journey in authoring this book. I would like to first like to thank our Lord and Savior for providing me with the courage to put my life into the written word and to tell my true story. My husband Shawn for tricking me into therapy so that I could figure out what this entire mess was all about. You are so forgiven, love.

I would be amiss if I did not thank Amy, Lorraine, and Danny for the encouragement along the way.

Lisa Oberg, my Nurse Practitioner, who keeps my mood and brain in the right place every couple of weeks. She's like a spa session to clear my aura.

My therapist in this big nightmare that brought me to light, Mirko Pavlek, who figured out my "society" and helped me to invite them to one big happy party that we call my life. I am forever indebted to you for your brilliance.

www.ingramcontent.com/pod-product-compliance
Lightning Source LLC
Chambersburg PA
CBHW021337160726
47994CB00007B/2736